YOU WERE BORN A BRAND

TEACHING FROM AN AWARD
WINNING BRAND MASTER

BY

LATANGELA F. SHERMAN

DEDICATION

Dedicated to my late Grandparents:
Reverend Jessie Lafayette, Sr.
And
Mrs. Olive Olivia Wright Lafayette
I can never thank you enough for the words of
encouragement you spoke into my life. I love you my angels.

To my Mother:
Rhonda Fay Lafayette Sherman
I admire your strength, your courage, your faith.
Thank you for guiding me along the way.
I love you.

I-722(4/30) = W.W.I.A.

CONTENTS

ACKNOWLEDGMENTS

Thank you to my family, friends and community that has supported and inspired my vision along this journey.

Branding Yourself And Your Business

Let's get it working for YOU!

We were all born a unique creation with special characterizations within. That uniqueness qualifies us as our own brand. Our minds hold the power to build us into anything we choose to accomplish. It is a driving force that only we have control of. We have the power to master our minds to solidify the brand we wish to portray. Just like all of God's creations, it starts with the foundation which leads to the structure, until all components are filled into our desired capacity. As we know, successful businesses doesn't happen overnight.

It takes years to establish from ground up using a plan that starts with the mastering of a mind that is determined to go through whatever obstacles it takes to achieve the dream. The dream that will take many levels of strategizing to process into your reality. In my early years of building, I've stirred many pots trying to brew up the perfect formula for a quick fix.

I've learned that there is no such quick fix to build a full functioning and successful business or service brand. If that was possible then we'd all be doing it. What a great world it would be. But with the rate of modern technology, I wouldn't rule it out down our future lines. As for now, we must take the routes available to us. Reach inside of your uniqueness and create your reality, which is your brand from within. Stay focused on the fact that branding is one of the most important drivers to sales when it comes to your business and products. Through your brand you could become globally successful and gain recognition for all of your hard work and efforts. Your uniqueness will make it difficult for the competitors to shadow your branding concepts. As you start from ground zero you will need a defined strategy that will help strengthen and identify your brand to stand out from the rest. That is very essential for a successful outcome.

Joshua 1:9 *Have I not commanded you? Be strong and courageous. Do not be terrified; do not be discouraged, for the LORD your God will be with you wherever you go.*

My 5 W's of Branding

It's not just that I'm a curious or nosey person. I just believe in asking questions about what I need to know. That's where these 5 W's comes into play. Asking these questions, not only to or for yourself, but also for the needs of your clients and associates in the industry or to those whom are interested in a brand pattern for their business needs to lay out in order to pinpoint whatever similarities, differences or adjustments that may be needed to structure their business plan. My clients come from all walks of life from different parts of the globe and they all have ideas of what they want to achieve for their own business success. No two minds think alike and that's where the 5 W's sets them all apart to recognize and customize each unique idea to create personalized profiles that will characterize each distinct brand to match the personality of the client and how they choose to bring attention to their brand to represent their business. Creating an impressive profile will set the stage for the customer. But it must reflect the true essence of the business.

With creativity of the imagination, it can take your business to a place that you could've only had wished to come true.

When branding yourself and your business the guideline of my 5 W's will serve as a road map for your clients of **WHO** you are; **WHAT** you are about; **WHEN** is the most effective time to bring you into their fold to enhance their operation; **WHERE** you are willing to take their vision and **WHY** you are the perfect fit for the job.

II Timothy 1:7 *For the Spirit God gave us does not make us timid, but gives us power, love and self-discipline.*

The courage we have within us could do amazing things and we should not be afraid to utilize it in the name of God. We shall fear no one but God and walk in His light with every step we take on our path to building our birth brand. We have the power to choose to stay in His guidance and not let the influence of bad marketing sway our direction of which seems to be an easier route.

You Must Be Consistent for there are many things we think of doing but it rarely gets much farther than just an idea if we don't make it a main factor of our goals and keep it in motion as we gather all the needed information to achieve the step by step process to begin to feed that idea into fruition.

Proverbs 3:13 *Happy is the man who finds wisdom, and the man who gains understanding.*

You Must Be Attentive to every aspect of your work in progress and beyond. It is your brain child that you would need to pamper and nurture throughout its growth. And with the growth that it will endure for as many years as its being nurtured, preservation is key for the longevity to carry on its functions for many generations and the potential opportunity of franchise possibilities as we see with many successfully operated brands.

You Must Be Persistent and never take "no" as a final answer as there will be quite a few no's to push through. There are many alternate routes to take. Let the discouragements become encouragements to know that as long as your idea is active, you are able to keep it in action. It's up to you to keep the force moving. After all its your dream. It's your life to change.

You Must Be Detailed and know all there is to know about your business and your brand. There should never be a question asked that you are unable to answer about what you have built. From the tiniest to the mega details you should have no hesitation or lack of knowledge about your creation.
The manifestation of your dream projects should be as vivid of a memory even a decade from when it was first put into motion of its first step of the building process. For if you believe in your brand it will show through your work to those who would consider you as the "*It Factor*" to seek for their branding needs.

Happy clients always refer others. Those moments of accomplishments are priceless and the details are forever etched in the heart and soul of the master behind the brand. This may seem like a simple thing but many of my clients have trouble when it comes to developing their unique personal branding method. They usually get overwhelmed thinking that they may not succeed at being different enough to stand out.

You can't be successful when you're always worrying about the competition as there are too many to compare to and you need to only focus on what you are building. The only thing that can affect you is to be distracted into losing focus. Your identity is as simple as who you are. So come up with a plan that will identify with you and your company as a personal brand.

Create something that will distinctively relate to what you are attracting attention to. What is the main product or focus of your business that will set you apart from companies selling similar products.

Do your research on other brands and see what characterizes their brand that impacts their success and you will realize that it's very conducive to something which represents them personally. It is important to define your own personal goals as the way you've envisioned for yourself according to the operations of your own business.

Being customized through plans that will brand you into whatever is being built for you are the representative of what you promote, therefore, you must evaluate your position within your industry to relate to what you are selling and promoting. Manage your brand in a way that works for you, because it's a problem in this saturated market to find a niche as a professional. Whether you're a self-employed entrepreneur, an executive at a large corporation or managing a small business, you will be in charge of and responsible for your own career.

Mark 8:36 *For what does it profit a man to gain the whole world and forfeit his soul?*

It's always in your best interest to have a track record that speaks on your behalf to prove your dedication and that you're a hard worker and a problem solver. This ability will speak volumes as a true visionary which is always needed on all levels of business when companies are in the face of challenges.

Be it an economic standstill, personal issues or the rise of competition in the market, there will always be room at the table for those who could create new positions and opportunities. This will contribute to long term success. That's how important the uniqueness of your brand will be to your approach. It will set you apart from the competitors and set the tone for more clientele to contribute to your brand's buy in.

Nothing is perfect but find the best ways possible to keep your brand consistent with its stories familiarity and of the special services it has to offer. There should never be a time that you don't believe in or stand behind all that you are advertising, because if you don't then it would make it hard for your customers to. It's great to have a reputable brand to stand firm on.

Your time is valuable and there will be those who don't respect that so it's up to you to take care of your own value which is your self- worth. It is all instilled within you. Your professional identity should be that thing that you do only the way that you can do it which personalizes your unique creations. Being confident will encourage you when you feel the pressures from all of the responsibilities of deadlines when time seems scarce. You should never let the work take control of you. Your clients should be able to sense your confidence as to who you are as their mentor, in order to trust your guidance with their vision as to what you could do to help and enhance their brand. They want to know that you are the right fit for their needs. It is a commitment until the job is done.

To be successful for the long haul of it, you must understand how important it is to be persistent with your approach. Your identity will set you apart from the competition and will contribute to the clientele's confidence with your brand.

Everything developed is a process.
There is something new developed every day so why not let it be something of yours. It's as simple as starting with yourself. You are your own person and the only you there will ever be. Your given birth name is your first form of a brand. That gift from the one who named you. You will be known by that brand forever. Whether you are on earth or long gone to your eternity, that name will linger to your next generation.
Create a brand that can be passed on through whatever you choose to develop today. These are the many memories to be made. Make it work to your advantage as this is your very own personal brand development.
When building my personal brand I developed a personal positioning statement within my body of work. You need specific characteristics and expertise to dominate in your industry. When asked "why should they choose you for the job?", you need a concise statement that highlights your unique values as a business professional.
You should even create a catchy slogan that captures who you are that makes you stand out from the competitors.

Do whatever you feel it takes to benefit your company because in marketing, consumers tends to favor the judgment of particular brands of products due to being bias towards the associations of people and their brands. This is what's called the "halo effect". Such as endorsements of their favorite celebrity or moguls they have looked up to since childhood.

Their influence sparks their interest even if they've never used the product.

The endorsement is enough to have them sold on it. It coincides with the uniqueness of their personal branding which keeps the consumers who are also their fans interested. This is why it's important to develop your very own personal brand so that your company also gets included in the positive halo of your success. Strategize a way to gain even more influence in your industry which will direct you to more connections and network sources in which those positive developments can be transferred to your company.

That effort to do good business for clients will keep finding its way back to you through associations and endorsements.

Numbers 23:19.. *God is not man, that he should lie, or a son of man, that he should change his mind. Has he said, and will he not do it? Or has he spoken, and will he not fulfill it?*

THE QUALITY OF YOUR BRAND

Find ways to perfect your version of personal branding. We choose one product over another because it either has something special to offer or renders a sense of familiarity. Maybe this brand is a part of my family tradition and I would like to carry it on… Maybe this brand caters to my habits of using shredded cheese -vs- chipped cheese. Develop a unique personal brand consistent with your story, your product, your pitch and your customer base will be just as consistent with the story and product that is mended within their lives as well.

What does it mean to brand yourself?

Setting yourself apart from others either in your company or in your industry with a special professional identity with "THAT THING" that you do only the way that you can do it, is a part of your personal branding.

With more responsibility on your plate, time becomes scarce. You may feel as if you do not have the time to allocate to building or managing your company's brand, or even your own.

You must commit to being the brand manager of your own personal brand.

I have found it very helpful in my line of work to develop a personal positioning statement within my body of work. Finding my specific characteristics and levels of expertise assisted me in dominating my industry. Focusing on being the right fit for the job by implementing attention to detail has served as a great value as a business professional.

Put some thought into creating a slogan of sorts that captures who you are and what sets you apart from the competition.

Branding yourself benefits your company! The connections that you make and the network that you develop can be transferred to your company. Make it an effort to do good business and be good to people...

The goodness will find its way back. Regardless of the level you are within your career, it is important to stay relevant, marketable and effective. You are the product and your employer is the customer. Brand yourself in such a way you are able to market your skills as a separate entity that will enhance any brand you attach yourself with. This gives you more opportunities for mobility both within and outside of your corporation. As you become more engaged with your brand expansion, you may be invited to speak at industry events, work with restructuring corporations and endless opportunities which may seem unimaginable at the moment; but your reputation will proceed you and the brand has spoken volumes….. You are prepared for the next phase of a wider industry.

An effective brand strategy gives you a major edge in increasingly competitive markets. But what exactly does "branding" mean? How does it affect a small business like yours?

Leviticus 19:14 *You shall not curse the deaf or put a stumbling block before the blind, but you shall fear your God: I am the Lord.*

Your brand is your solid word to your customer. It tells them what they can expect from your products and services, and it differentiates your offering from your competitors'. Your brand is an example of who you are, who you want to be and who people perceive you to be.

How do you see yourself? Are you the experienced reliable source? Or are you the innovative quick on the spot, wing it as I go wiz kid?

Who you are should be based to some extent on who your target customers want and need you to be. Decide if your product is the high-cost, high-quality option, or the lower-cost, higher-value option.

You cannot be both and you cannot be everything to everyone.

In order to solidify your place within your industry, you must communicate your brand. Define your brand in such a way, it is understood every encounter shall be as consistent as the last or the next.

Questions that need answers:

Do you have a personal brand management strategy?
Communicate with others your pinpointed unique brand. Express your vision you're your team and keep in mind that actively promoting and managing your personal brand should be a goal. Consistency is pivotal, especially with the quick turn around on information through so many digital outlets.

Questions that need answers:

If you were to search your name on the internet today, what would you find?

Elementary as the question may seem, the answers holds a major key. Your clients are researching you before contacting you.
It would be a shame to lose potential clients due to the lack of maintaining a positive image consistent with the brand your company provides being displayed properly.

Control your online brand image by creating a personal website or a blog. Outline your achievements, share your distinct industry-related ideas. Become the market leader within your industry and set the pace.

 Invite other like-minded individuals to join in on the conversation and control the tone of the dialogue for an opportunity to network and expand your brand.

Your brand strategy is how, what, where, when and to whom you plan on communicating and delivering on your brand's messages.

Your distribution channels are also an important part of your brand strategy.

Questions that need answers:

Who arc you talking to?

Where you advertise is part of determining a large percentage of who you are delivering your message to. Place focus on what you communicate verbally and visually as a part of your brand strategy.

Setting yourself apart from the competition will strengthen the equity of your brand. Added value brought to your company's product and services will allow you to charge more for what you bring to the table. Unbranded products becomes the generic version. You'll find that customers will pay the worth of the brand as they are able to equate the value which is associated with the brand. The added value to brand equity frequently comes in the form of perceived quality or an emotional attachment. For example, major brand shoes associates its products with star athletes, understanding that customers will transfer an emotional attachment from the athlete to the product. Although the shoe may be an amazing product as is, it's not just the shoe's features that sell the shoe. Attaching a brand to a brand creates a super brand with astonishing sales. Leaving others to negotiate deals and form partnerships to enhance their product to stay relevant in attempts to keep up with the market.

LEVITICUS 19:13..

You shall not oppress your neighbor or rob him. The wages of a hired servant shall not remain with you all night until the morning.

<u>*BRANDSHIPS*</u> – The merging of brands to enhance individual growth as a collaborative venture.

As you develop a brand strategy, it helps to start at the beginning. In other words, begin by setting your business goals.
Why are you creating a new brand?
What do you hope to achieve by launching the new brand? Use those long-term objectives as a basis for all of your strategic branding efforts.
For example, are you trying to reach a new audience? Your brand strategy for achieving that goal is likely to be quite different from a business that wants to steal market share from a category leader, and that's why goal definition is a fundamental starting point for any brand strategy. One of the first questions you have to answer is, "Why?"

It's easy to get caught up in the short-term activities and tactics that drive business today, but when it comes to building a brand, that's a big mistake.

Brands aren't built overnight, so your brand strategy shouldn't be focused on short-term tactics but rather on long-term goals and sustainable growth.

With so many working parts to keeping business successful across the board, it can become challenging to stay strategic when executives are weighed down by data and demand measurable growth right now. The best brand leaders, however, fight against short-term focus, because they know being short-sighted is a brand killer.

As a brand manager or agency account planner, focus on being tactics driven. A high percentage of the daily processes within marketing departments and ad agencies are based in project management. Be a brand manager that works hand in hand with your communication partners to focus on the best way to manage, process and organize the tight budgets allocated to maximize visibility of the brand on the minimal side of the budget.

Building a solid brand will allow you be consistent with marketing. Being able to deliver the same message of what your brand's promise is to the client. Thinking long-term when at the crossroads of strategic and creative decision-making is important for the relevancy of your brand. Of course you should be focused on getting a job done in a timely fashion and within a certain budget. However, keeping an open mind on where the next phase of the plan will lead is pivotal in staying ahead of the curb. Instead of focusing on short-term tactics, become brand architects which enables teams to design a lasting structure that will bridge brand strategy and brand messaging. Without a strong brand foundation built on a well-defined strategy, brands have little chance for success.

Leviticus 19:11 *You shall not steal; you shall not deal falsely; you shall not lie to one another.*

GIVE YOUR BRAND AN IDENTITY

The quality of your brand is consistent with the fiber of which it stems.

Be honest in all you do and you will gain a reputation that will keep your clients recommending other clients which will continue to grow your business. One of the best organic flow of clientele that will continuously work in your favor.

While attempting to define your brand, dedicate time to do your research, fine tune your message and create answers to the following questions...

What is your company's mission?

What qualities do you want them to associate with your company?

What do your customers and prospects already think of your company?

What are the benefits and features of your products or services?

Do your research. Learn the needs, habits and desires of your current and prospective clients. Don't rely on what you think they think. Know what they think.

And never be afraid to reach out to business mentors for sound advice.

Linking the core of your brand with an extension of visual branding is an intricate step as well.

Get a great logo!

A logo that will stand boldly with the vision of your definition is a major advantage.

The design, the color the font. Let it be a cohesive piece that serves as a reflection of your brand. Something you are willing to stand behind.

The foundation of your brand is your logo.

Your website, packaging and promotional materials--all of which should integrate your logo works hand in hand with the consistency of the branding you present.

Once you've defined your brand, how do you get the word out?

Radio; Television; Print; Word of mouth…

How do you plan to deliver your message?

Building a successful brand is about more than designing a cool logo and being known for flashing a members only jacket.

Many brands miss the mark at what they are trying to accomplish. Most people think of branding as simply "the logo," but a logo is just the beginning of a brand's visual aspect which also includes the website, marketing materials, and ad copy — which in turn includes tag lines, marketing/PR/sales copy, and advertisements.

Importantly, a brand's visual elements are only half of the story. Less tangible assets such as corporate culture, how the executive team and even how employees conduct themselves are all part of a brand's fiber.

Formulate a plan that will work seamlessly with your attempts to reach your targeted demographic.

Write down your brand messaging.

Habakkuk 2:2 *And the LORD answered me, and said, Write the vision, and make it plain upon tables, that he may run that readeth it.*

What are the key messages you want to communicate about your brand?

Every employee should be aware of your brand attributes as they are reflections of what your brand entails.

Branding extends to every aspect of your business from how you answer your phones, what you or your salespeople wear on sales calls, even your e-mail signature.

The "voice" for your company should reflect your brand. This voice should be applied to all written communication and incorporated in the visual imagery of all materials, online and off.

What is the tone of your brand's voice? Is your brand friendly? Be conversational. Is it regional? Be more customized to the details.

Develop a tagline.

Write a memorable, meaningful and concise statement that captures the tone of your brand.

Design templates and create brand standards for your marketing materials. Use the same color scheme, logo placement, look and feel throughout. Sometimes, we may feel overwhelmed to go over the top and be super fancy.

The truth is, you don't need to be fancy, just consistent.

Be true to your brand. Customers won't return to you--or refer you to someone else--if you don't deliver on your brand promise.

The marketing practice of creating a name, symbol or design that identifies and differentiates a product from other products. An effective brand strategy gives you a major edge in increasingly competitive markets. ... Simply put, your brand is your promise to your customer.

Be consistent. Being consistent is one of the most important tips I can give you. If you can't do this, your attempts at establishing a brand will fail.

A long-term plan for the development of a successful brand in order to achieve specific goals is definitely needed.

A well-defined and executed brand strategy affects all aspects of a business and is directly connected to consumer needs, emotions, and competitive environments.

Proverbs 22:1 *A good name is to be chosen rather than great riches, and favor is better than silver or gold.*

Brand attributes portray a company's brand characteristics. They signify the basic nature of your brand. Brand attributes are a bundle of features that highlight the physical and personality aspects of the brand. The tone of your brand is developed through images, actions, or presumptions. Brand attributes help in creating brand identity.

Proverbs 11:14 *Without the guidance of good leaders a nation falls. But many good advisers can save it.*

To be a good leader you must know how to give and receive advice that is beneficial to the well- being of your company and clients. Constructive criticism should always be welcome and we must agree to disagree. Communication is necessary in any relationship of the meeting of the minds.

Your team's focus should be on helping to build success just as much as it is your focus. We all know that team work makes the dream work.

A strong brand must consist of:

Relevancy- A strong brand must be relevant. It must meet people's expectations and should perform the way they want it to. A good job must be done to persuade consumers to buy the product; make your product unique.

Uniqueness- A strong brand should be different and unique. It should set you apart from other competitors in market.

Consistency- A consistent brand signifies what the brand stands for and builds customers trust in brand. A consistent brand is where the company communicates messages in a way that does not deviate from the core brand proposition.

Sustainable- A strong brand makes a business competitive. A sustainable brand drives an organization towards innovation and success.

Credibility- A strong brand should do what it promises. The way you communicate your brand to the customers should be realistic. It should not fail to deliver what it promises. Do not exaggerate as customers want to believe in the promises you make to them. Do not over promise and under deliver. They will remember.

Proper positioning- A strong brand should be positioned so that it makes a place in target audience mind and they prefer it over other brands.

Inspirational- A strong brand should transcend and inspire the category it is conncctcd to.

Appealing- A strong brand should be attractive. Customers should be attracted by the promise you make and by the value you deliver.

Brand management begins with having a thorough knowledge of the term "brand". It includes developing a promise, making that promise and maintaining it.
Concentrating on defining the brand, positioning the brand, and delivering the brand. Brand management is nothing but the process of creating and sustaining the brand. Branding makes customers committed to your business.

A strong brand differentiates your products from the competitors. It gives a quality image to your business.
Brand management includes managing the tangible and intangible characteristics of brand. In case of product brands, the tangibles include the product itself, as well as the other factors such as price, packaging and even includes the customers' experience.
The intangibles include emotional connections with the product and the service. BRANDING will give you and your product an identity. It is nothing but capturing your customers attention with your brand name. It gives an image of an experienced, steady and reliable business.

It is all about capturing the niche market for your product or service and creating a confidence in the current and prospective customers' minds that you are the unique solution to their issues at hand.

The aim of branding is to convey a vivid message, create a loyal relationship with you and your client base, persuade the buyer for the product, and establish an emotional connectivity with the consumers.

Branding forms customer perceptions about the product. It should raise customer expectations about the product. The primary aim of branding is to set you apart from the competition in the best way possible.

A customer with a strong connection of familiarity in a brand, will spend faster and refer to others on the relief the brand has brought to them. The customers can better imagine the intangible goods with the help of brand name. Strong brand organizations have a high market share. The brand should be given good support so that it can sustain itself in the long run. It is essential to manage all brands and build brand equity over a period of time.

A successful brand can only be created if the brand management system is competent. Brand management helps in building a corporate image. A brand manager has to oversee overall brand performance and stick to the plan in order to take things to the next level.

- Brand Development Strategy for Your Professional Services

Your brand is perhaps your professional services most valuable asset. If this is true, then developing a stronger brand is your most important task. Leave little room as possible for error on the basis of what is to be expected from your brand.

A professional service brand is best understood as your firm's reputation and it's visibility in the marketplace. Keep in mind your ability to strengthen your brand increases when you build a strong, consistent reputation and visibility within your area of expertise.

I Corinthians 9:24.. *Do you not know that in a race all the runners run, but only one gets the prize? Run in such a way as to get the prize.*

Maintaining your visibility within the marketplace is of great importance, but keep in mind that your reputation often makes its way around a lot faster. Gain strength within your field of being one of good character, doing good work and with consistency.

Are you prepared to meet the needs of the client according to the presentation and core foundation of your brand?
Brand development is the process of creating and strengthening your professional services brand. As we help firms develop their brands, we divide the process into several phases.

• **Getting their brand strategy right and aligned with their business objectives.**

• **Developing all the tools they will need to communicate their brand**

• **Strengthening their newly developed or updated brand.**

Habakkuk 2:3 *But these things I plan won't happen right away. Slowly, steadily, surely, the time approaches when the vision will be fulfilled. If it seems slow, do not despair, for these things will surely come to pass. Just be patient! They will not be overdue a single day.*

BRANDING BUILDING BLOCKS

Identifying Your Lane

Who are your target clients? If you say "everybody" you are making a very big mistake. My time spent researching clearly showed me that high growth, high profit firms are focused on having clearly defined target clients. The narrower the focus, the faster the growth. The more diverse the target audience, the more diluted your marketing efforts will be. So how do you know if you have chosen the right target client group?
Your brand development strategy is how you go about accomplishing a few branding tasks.

Let Your Brand Cater To You

Proverbs 3:5-6 *Trust in the Lord with all your heart. Lean not on your own understanding, in all your ways acknowledge him, and he will direct your path.*

- Identify your brand positioning.

Determine your firm's brand positioning within the professional services marketplace. Working on your market positioning is a top priority. How is your firm different from others and why should potential clients within your target audience choose to work with you?

A positioning statement is typically three to five sentences in length and captures the essence of your brand positioning. It must be grounded in reality, as you will have to deliver on what you promise. It must also be a bit aspirational so you have something to strive for.

- Research your target client group.

Being a firm that conducts systematic research on your target client group will help you grow faster and to become more profitable. Once you have found your groove, continue researching your market and targeted areas, keeping your creative wheels turning and remain competitive. Becoming comfortable will allow you to miss the shift.

Research helps you understand your target client's perspective and priorities, anticipate their needs and put your message in language that resonates with them. It also tells you how they view your firm's strengths and your current brand. Remain focused on growing your brand as a continuous evolution, inspiring your clients to evolve as well.

- Consider your overall business strategy.

Have a concrete overall business strategy in place. Your brand development strategy depends on a solid foundation. A strong brand will make growing your firm a lot easier.
If you are clear about where you want to take your business, your brand will help you get there.

Colossians 3:17 *And whatever you do, in word or deed, do everything in the name of the Lord Jesus, giving thanks to God the Father through him.*

- Develop your messaging strategy.

Your next step is a messaging strategy that translates your brand positioning into messages to your various target audiences. Your target audiences typically include potential clients, potential employees, referral sources or other influencers and potential partnering opportunities, to name a few. While your core brand positioning must be the same for all audiences, each audience will be interested in different aspects of it. The messages to each audience will emphasize the most relevant points. Each audience will also have specific concerns that must be addressed, and each will need different types of evidence to support your messages. Your messaging strategy should address all of these needs. This is an important step in making your brand relevant to your target audiences.

John 16:33 *I have told you these things, so that in me you may have peace. In this world you will have trouble. But take heart! I have overcome the world.*

- Develop your virtual platform.

Your website is your single most important brand development tool. It is where all your audiences turn to learn what you do, how you do it and who your clients are. Prospective clients are not likely to choose your firm solely based on your website. But they may rule you out if your site sends the wrong message.

It is very important to pay attention to the content displayed pertaining to your brand. Developing a website allows you to place uniformed content for clients to familiarize themselves with you, your work and platform. Your website will be home to your content. Be conscious of the information you place within your site and link effective search engine triggers. The focus of your search engine optimization efforts should be so precise that your prospects, potential employees, and referral sources will find you and learn about your firm. Online presence is one of the fastest growing tools used today. While building your marketing toolkit, keep in mind your site should convey who you are, who you serve and exactly what you do.

Use your brand message as an introduction and selling point.

The next step in the process is to build out the remainder of your marketing toolkit. This might include one-page "sales sheets" that describe core services offerings or key markets served. It is perfectly fine to give generic information and encourage clients to contact you for a customized package as each case has its individual needs.

Give and overview of your firm or key offerings, an e-brochure or testimonials from past clients that have worked with the firm. Key services offerings are also very useful. If prepared appropriately, these tools serve not only a business development function but also are important for brand development.

II Peter 1:3.. *His divine power has granted to us all things that pertain to life and godliness, through the knowledge of him who called us to his own glory and excellence.*

For many firms, a name change is not required. But if you are a new firm, are undergoing a merger or are dealing with a name that no longer suits your positioning, a name change may be in order.

Remember, your name, logo and tagline are not your brand. They are ways to communicate or symbolize your brand. While forming ideas or transitioning do not make the mistake of showing the new logo around internally to get a consensus. The name, logo and tagline are not for you. They are for your marketplace and should be judged on how well they communicate, not how much the partners like them.

Live it and make it real!

Philippians 4:13.. *I can do all things through Christ who strengthens me.*

- Develop your content marketing strategy.

Content marketing is particularly well suited to professional services firms within the internet world. It does all things traditional marketing does but it is capable of doing them more efficiently. It uses valuable educational content to attract, nurture and qualify prospects.
Remember that your brand strength is driven by both visibility and reputation. Increasing visibility alone, without strengthening your reputation, is rarely successful. That's why traditional awareness-building advertising or sponsorships so often yield disappointing results.
On the other hand, content marketing increases both visibility and reputation at the same time. It is also the perfect way to make your brand relevant to your target audiences. Become an integrated part of the lifestyle portrayed by your targeted audience.
Customize your approach and allow the simple steps with consistency etch your mark.

- Implement, track, and adjust.

A very important step in the brand development process is to implement ideas and strategies that may be productive towards making an impact. Taking different approaches will allow you to track results and weigh options on which may have been best effective. Having the ability to adjust allows you to identify a better method and can save you lots of time, play a role with damage control and even protect revenue.

Obviously a winning brand development strategy doesn't do much good if it is never implemented. You might be surprised at how often that happens. A solid strategy is developed and started with all the good intentions the firm can muster. Then reality intervenes. People get busy with client work and brand development tasks get put off... then forgotten.

That's why tracking is so important. I strongly recommend tracking both the implementation of the plan as well as results. Did the strategy get implemented as planned?

What happened with the objective measures, such as search traffic and web visitors?

How many new leads, employee applications and partnering opportunities were generated? Only by tracking the entire process can you make sure you are drawing the right conclusions and making the right adjustments. The outburst of digital marketing has made it nearly impossible to thrive in the marketplace without giving some serious thought towards "digital campaigning".

Social networking websites allow individuals, businesses and other organizations to interact with one another and build relationships and communities online. Allowing you an unlimited resource of information on trends, outlets to connect with brands which reflects upon yours and your tribe. When companies join these social channels, consumers can interact with them directly. It gives the client a bird's eye view of the work you have done and a guideline as of what they can expect to receive from your services. That interaction can be more personal to users than traditional methods of outbound marketing and advertising.

With the use of social networking sites acting as a faster medium of word of mouth or more precisely, e-word of mouth, the internet has the ability to reach billions across the globe and contains a powerful impact.

The internet is a prime example of an influence network. It can effect buying patterns and product or service acquisition. Social networking sites and blogs allow followers to become more interactive with the ability to "retweet" or "repost" comments made by others about a product being promoted, which occurs quite frequently on some social media sites. Because the information about the product is being put out there and is getting repeated, more traffic is brought to the brand attached.

Social networking websites are based on building virtual communities that allows your tribe to express their needs, wants, values and even their opinions online.

Social media marketing also connects consumers and audiences to businesses that share the same needs, wants, and values.

Through social networking sites, companies can keep in touch with individual followers. With the correct product placement social media presents an upper hand to brands that may not have a large marketing budget, but may have a creative tactic that sparks interest to give the brand a massive boost.

By choosing whom to follow on these sites, products can reach a very narrow target audience. Social networking sites also include much information about what products and services prospective clients might be interested in.

Through the use of new analysis technologies, marketers can detect buying signals, such as content shared by people and questions posted online. An understanding of buying signals can help sales people target relevant prospects and marketers run micro-targeted campaigns. Your digital imprints with every follow of a page, click on a link or comment on a post sends alerts to market analysts.

Creating a strong sense of online awareness for your brand or the products of your clients is a very competitive method to blaze the market.

Work towards building a strong brand development process to drive the growth and profitability of your business.

Discover your true differentiators and give clients a reason to pick you out of the crowd. Staying flexible with the ability to adapt will always give you an edge.

Of course, the best brands stick with their strategies, but those strategies leave room for flexibility as the market, consumers, and competitors change.

Remember:

Just as your goals in life might change over time, so might your brand goals.

Similarly, just as you might modify your plan to achieve your goals in life, so too might your brand marketing plan change.

G.O.A.L.S. = **G**oing **O**ver **A**ll **L**ittle **S**teps

Finally, just as you seize opportunities to move closer to your goals as they arise throughout your life, you'll also seize short-term opportunities to grow your brand and move closer to achieving your long-term brand goals as those opportunities are presented to you.

A specific, achievable brand strategy is an essential component of any business, because it affects every area of your business.

Leviticus 19:10 *And you shall not strip your vineyard bare, neither shall you gather the fallen grapes of your vineyard. You shall leave them for the poor and for the sojourner: I am the Lord your God.*

YOUR BRAND IS YOUR IMAGE

Personal branding is the practice of people marketing themselves and their careers as brands. Personal branding is essentially the ongoing process of establishing a prescribed image or impression in the mind of others about an individual, group, or organization. Personal branding often involves the application of one's name to various products. Your brand can be thought of as a perception or emotion, maintained by somebody other than yourself that describes the experience of having a relationship with you.

The relationship between brands and consumers needs to be constantly made and remade, and this continuous process creates a demonstration of the growth in brand cultures.

This same logic follows for personal brands as there is a constant desire for a reinforcement of the self-brand.

Branding has reached a new level of imperative because of the rise of the virtual world. It has created the necessity of managing online identities.

Despite being expressly virtual, social media and online identity has the ability to affect the real world.

Because individuals want to portray themselves a certain way to their social circle, they may work to maintain a certain image on their social media sites. As a result, social media enables the creation of an online identity that may not be completely true to the real self. Displaying why it is important for the consistency of your brand to flow in writing and in action. Employers are now increasingly using social media tools in order to review applicants before offering them interviews. Such techniques range from searching the applicants Facebook Or Twitter feed to conducting large background checks using search engines and other tools. Your brand is your resume to potential clients and partners. Use your brand to provide potential employers with access to a number of personal brand assets. Show your ability to brand control by holding your personal brand to the highest level possible at all times.

A brand is a promise to the market and a means to differentiate yourself from competition.

As a promise, your brand says, "When in doubt, this is what you can expect from us." As a means of differentiation, a brand says, "All things being equal, you're safer with us." Unfortunately, too many business professionals think that "brand" is a "marketing thing" when, in fact, a brand is the result of a customer support call, a sales promise, the quality of an update, the courteousness of a delivery, and virtually everything else a company does.
Brand is, in fact, the essence of the business.

The characteristics of an organization should focus on leadership, teamwork, keeping the morale high, encouraging high performance and maintaining structure. Your brand should have a secure sense of those that it represents and have the ability to adapt to what may need to be provided in order to keep the brand loyal to the promise of being consistent to the needs of the client.
It is important that those within the organization value their positions. This results in productivity for the organization and loyalty among members.

Members should also be provided with the opportunity to advance within the organization, which fuels motivation.

An organization is likely to fail without a strong sense of leadership. Become a brand that promotes growth within the organization. Management should maintain a strong relationship with members, who should be given a firm sense of direction. Branding leadership and exemplifying teamwork begins within and is extended to those joining the fold.

Management should effectively communicate with members and provide them with knowledge needed to perform the organization's required tasks.

Teamwork is also important within an organization. The organization's members should share common goals and work together to reach them.

Teams may be developed within the organization, each working toward a shared goal of enhancing the brand.

Performance should be a priority in any organization.

Exceptional performance can result in awards for individuals or teams within an organization to help encourage good work. Poor performance should be addressed quickly and corrected. Constructive criticism is highly important to a successful organization. Managing your brand on a personal note will prepare you to elevate *brandships* as they form.

An organization without a defined structure is likely to fail. An organization's goals, mission and vision should be clearly defined. It is easier for members to follow management's requests when they understand the reasoning behind them. It is important that the structure of the organization does not limit possibilities for future growth.

A strong, well differentiated brand will make growing your firm much easier. But what type of firm do you want? Are you planning to grow organically? Your overall business strategy is the context for your brand development strategy, so that's the place to start. If you are clear about where you want to take your brand, your brand will help you get there.

Brand building is an integral aspect of personal and business development. It not only increases the voice and consumer awareness of a brand, but it also gives it an identity and worth. If you have been thinking of building a personal or business brand, then it is important for you to know that brand building takes a great deal of time, research and resources.

Looking at the different types of brands and the steps to create a successful brand you will begin to realize there is no one set definition that actually captures the true essence of brand building in its entirety. Many people think that brand building is all about communicating and exposing your brand. That is just one side of it. The best way I can define it is that it is a process of creating value to consumers and catering to their needs with a customized approach with attention to detail. It encompasses all things that consumers know, feel, and experience about your business as a whole.

Know where you stand…Know who you are!
Within your marketplace, define your role.
How would you best describe your brand
from the options below?

Are you a **Service brand**? This brand is built
on knowledge, culture, and experience that
one has with the service delivering
agency/company/people.

Would you fall more so under the category of
a **Retail brand**? This brand is built on a
mixture of products and service experience.
Or would you say that your level of expertise
serves as a **Product brand**? This brand is
built on the experience that one has with a
specific product.

The first stage in brand building is defining
your brand. This is a very critical step as it
ultimately determines what your brand truly
stands for. When defining your business
brand, you should create a checklist of its core
strengths. Similarly, if you're defining a
personal brand, you should look at the skills
and expertise that you possess especially those
which stand out. Your values should in one
way or another show that you are contributing
to environmental, social, and economic well-
being of consumers.

You may not realize some of these important aspects of brand building immediately, until you look at them objectively.

Isaiah 43:19 *Behold, I am doing something new! It's already happening; don't you recognize it? I will clear a way in the desert. I will make rivers on dry land.*

A pure service brand is a brand that creates services that have no significant tangible aspect to them. A good example of this would be that of a water park. Companies can make products or services. Products are tangible things that you can own. The company that makes your cell phone has made an item that you can pick up, hold, use.

Philippians 4:6 *Do not be anxious about anything, but in everything, by prayer and petition, with thanksgiving, present your requests to God.*

- Personalize your Brand

If you want your brand building campaign or brand to be successful, then you have to personalize it. I cannot express enough how important it is to give your brand an identity. Let consumers see and experience the personality of your brand in its entirety. Look at your brand as something that a consumer wants to identify with pretty much as they would with their favorite cars, shoes, or electronics.

- Expose your Brand

Building a unique and powerful personal or business brand takes time and consistency. To build your personal brand, you have to keep reinforcing your values and skills by taking up new roles and assignments that will give you more exposure. Facebook, LinkedIn, Twitter, Instagram, to name a few are some of the most popular social media platforms used to create, maintain and harbor the voice for your personal or business brand.

The things people think, know and say about you will motivate people to identify and join with your brand.

When building your brand, you should also endeavor to develop brand personality. The truth is; if you execute your brand building strategies consistently, then you will easily establish a pattern that will forever be associated with your brand name.

• Customizing Advertisement

If you were to create a face for your business to help people remember you, would it add some humor or personality to the brand that could be considered a functional brand expansion?

Is your product or service one that could benefit the use of animation or would it take away from the message of what your targeted audience really desires?

Colossians 3:23 *Whatever you do, work heartily, as for the Lord and not for men.*

- Position Your Brand

Before embarking on brand building, you have to take time to differentiate it so that you can attract attention and stand out from competitors. To differentiate your brand, you have to create a unique advantage in the mind of consumers not merely getting attention by brand building colors or logos or other superficial elements. Once you come up with a unique value proposition, you should use a good branding strategy to position your brand in a way that will help consumers see and appreciate the greater value of your brand over competing ones in the market.

As you engage in brand building, you should also invite customers to be co-creators of brand values so that they can feel that they also own it and relate with it. Create some type of buy-in that will encourage consumer-brand interaction by personalizing products to meet the needs and preferences of consumers. When you personalize your brand, you give consumers reason to participate and engage with your brand for a lifetime.

- Evaluate Your Brand

Your brand will go through a range of motions within its duration. Depending on your brand strategies, your brand will either grow in strength, or remain dormant, or recede with time. In the brand cycle, new events, changes, and circumstances bring challenges and opportunities to enhance the value of your brand or re-establish it. All these possibilities should give you the urge to take charge of your brand building activities.

As your brand name grows, so do the responsibilities and expectations to continue with brand building. Now is not the time to coast. Find ways to keep your creative wheels spinning.

The best way of ensuring brand growth is reviewing your activities and evaluating your successes through levels of brand awareness and levels of engagements. Allow yourself to be free enough to seize and exploit new opportunities while upholding your commitment to remain true to your vision and brand strategy. It will also help you steer your brand in the right direction and keep it relevant as you move into the future.

You have to define your brand, differentiate, present it, and review what your brand stands for from time to time. It is very important to be clear about your branding strategies and how you're going to implement them.
Becoming a market leader is one task, remaining a market leader is another. Each task requires new goals.
Going **O**ver **A**ll **L**ittle **S**teps to maintain a level of excellence and resilience to thrive within the market.
You should also adopt brand strategies that will add value to your consumers and help them develop the right impression of your company and what it truly stands for.

Proverbs 23:7 *As I think in my heart, so am I.*

• Share your ideas.

Be confident with sharing your ideas, beliefs, philosophy, methods and message. The more you place the word of your best thinking, the more you'll become known for your ideas.

- Batters Up

Create a quick pitch that effectively communicates what you want to be known for in a way that makes it easy for other people to talk about it. It is how you might introduce yourself to someone you just met in a lobby to get their attention. Shine such a level of confidence that they feel compelled to inquire more about you.

- Boost your profile

You need to amplify your profile both online and in traditional media. It is not about feeding your ego, it is about sharing your ideas with more people. The more seen, known and recognized you are, the more opportunity will flow your way. Encourage other like-minded individuals to join your journey.

You need to align yourself with the right mix of products and services. Great entrepreneurs and leaders are able to make excellent choices when it comes to what they sell. Make, source, innovate, reinvent and find unique and valuable ways to deliver your value.

LOYALTY IS THE ROYALTY OF YOUR BRAND

Brand Loyalty is a scenario where the consumer fears purchasing and consuming product from another brand which he does not trust. It is measured a great deal through familiarity, methods like word of mouth publicity, repetitive buying, price sensitivity, commitment, brand trust and customer satisfaction. Brand loyalty is the extent to which a consumer constantly buys the same brand within a product category.

Building brands and delivering value to the customers is one of the most interesting jobs that you can enjoy in marketing. What are some of the brands you purchase and would have a hard time replacing without a second thought? We associate products with the image of the brand, the logo and our connection with it.

When consumers are brand loyal they love "you" for being "you", and they will minutely consider any other alternative brand or person as a replacement.

Some examples of brand loyalty can be seen with the makes and models of vehicles, foods and beverages and hotel chains. Certain brands reign supreme with clients due to the way it has been integrated into their lifestyle. The brand has provided a certain level of comfort and certainty for them and enhanced an experience of some sort.

Brand loyal consumers are the foundation of an organization. Greater loyalty levels lead to less marketing expenditure because the brand loyal customers promote the brand positively. At some point, loyal customers also create a spring board of launching and introducing more products that are targeted at same customers at less expenditure. It also restrains new competitors in the market. Brand loyalty is a key component of brand equity.

Brand loyalty can be developed through various measures such as quick service, ensuring quality products, continuous improvement and a wide distribution network.

Brand loyalty can be defined as relative possibility of customer shifting to another brand in case there is a change in product's features, price or quality.

As brand loyalty increases, customers will respond less to competitive moves and actions. Brand loyal customers remain committed to the brand, are willing to pay higher price for that brand, and will promote their brand always.

There are many facets to marketing and selling apart from having to focus only on selling the product.

A company having brand loyal customers will have greater sales, less marketing and advertising costs, and best pricing.

This is because the brand loyal customers are less reluctant to shift to other brands, respond less to price changes and self- promote the brand as they perceive that their brand have unique value which is not provided by other competitive brands.

Brand loyalty is always developed post purchase. To develop brand loyalty, an organization should know their niche market, target them, support their product, ensure easy access of their product, provide customer satisfaction, bring constant innovation in their product and offer schemes on their product so as to ensure that customers repeatedly purchase the product.

Luke 12:48 *But he that knew not and committed things worthy of stripes, shall be beaten with few stripes. For unto whomsoever much is given, of him shall much be required; and to whom men have committed much, of him they will ask the more.*

- Creating BRANDSHIPS

Actively pursue partnerships with other influential brands and people that have the respect and trust of your target market. By association, their brand rubs off on your brand. You get to rapidly accelerate how you build, reach and trust with the people who matter in your industry. Forming those BRANDSHIPS will allow the merging of brands to enhance individual growth as a collaborative venture.

Focus on building a personal brand that yields true influence in your industry.

We seek respect in our professional lives. Gaining the respect of others in the workplace is something many people want, but often have misguided ideas on how to achieve this goal.

Hebrews 12:11 *No discipline seems pleasant at the time, but painful. Later on, however, it produces a harvest of righteousness and peace for those who have been trained by it.*

If you are unsure of the direction you want to go with your business, do not make a move until you make a plan, as you cannot build without the foundation. Respect the power of a plan. Failing to plan is a plan to fail. Making the prior preparations needed to prevent poor performance is necessary. Understanding your level of expertise, the challenges you may be facing within the market, the angle you should effectively approach first and aligning your efforts will give you a solid starting point to build.

Do not rush because that usually ends up with much left undone. Take the time to think and research all aspects of what you have your mind set on. Don't let the pressures of a start-up intimidate you, stay prepared, and never give up.

There is no need to race. Nor should you be anxious to get the job done.

In successful business, it is a wise decision to keep the pace of a steady process to stay focused on which you are building and meet the demands as they come. In God's perfect timing you will be ready to unveil your brand. What is the emotional reaction you want your audience to have when connecting the brand and what do you want them to remember? Develop your tagline based on this discussion. Develop your company's culture. And then do all your hiring and your onboarding with this culture in mind. Once you have established the tone of your brand's voice, do not bring on people who could destroy client relationships you spent months or years to cultivate. It only takes one customer's bad experience with one bad employee to sabotage a multimillion-dollar investment and throw away countless invested hours.

What are your top competitors doing to make their mark on the market and how are they expressing themselves? Look for some core similarities, and simultaneously prepare to identify where you can innovate and differentiate. Stand out from the crowd.

Think about who your audience is.

Be patient with your brand.

Take on every new outreach initiative with care. Don't be in a rush to take on more than you can chew. Take your time with any of your outreach activities, be it advertising or marketing materials.

Be consistent. Think of your outreach as an extension of your office, coworkers, clients and brand overall. The brand is the brain. Public relations, advertising, marketing, and sales are all extensions of that brain, and they must be coordinated and aligned. The copy, design and language your team uses is must always be based off of the brand. Remind yourself that it is indeed okay to get help. Branding is not easy. If it were, there would be a much greater number of stronger brands in the small business community.

The reason the market controllers of the world can have strong brands is because they have the dollars to spend on it.

But they weren't always conglomerates; if they can achieve brand success, so can you. First, you have to nail down step one: your brand!

A professional can take you through the process so you see things more clearly, get a different perspective, and go about branding in a way that will allow you to reach your market more efficiently.

I Thessalonians 5:16-19 *Be joyful always; pray continually; give thanks in all circumstances; this is the will of God for your life.*

Sheer talent can help you get your business going, your brand is what will sustain it.

II Timothy 3:16 *All Scripture is breathed out by God and profitable for teaching, for reproof, for correction, and for training in righteousness.*

EMBRACE THE HIGHS AND LOWS

Embracing failure might not be the first thing that springs to mind when it comes to branding tips but it is a very critical part of the brand-building process, and is a way your firm may learn valuable lessons from a brand personality that failed.

In such a copycat – me too society, it is almost impossible to find a marketplace that isn't crowded anymore, so you have to try to stand out from the competition to be remembered by customers and in the right way.

Find ways to customize your message while not losing the message.

Never lose sight of what the customers really wanted; excellent service, fast delivery and the best possible prices.

Your goal should always center around the purpose of making it easy for the customer.

Those values are represented in everything the company does, and it adds more value to the business than you know.

With brands it might be important if the brand is aspirational and needs to fit into a particular lifestyle, but if your business provides something customers need, rather than want, then prices and service may well be more important than brand personality.
Know your market and believe in your brand.
Trust the feedback of your experiences.
The surge in sales or the lack thereof are indicators of your hit and miss strategies.
Create a plan that will allow you to successfully test the market for an organic movement that will warrant you information that will spring you forward in the future.
 Every idea may not be a smash hit the first time around, but knowing when to swing at the pitch at the correct time makes the game changing play. Study the game.
 Prepare yourself and your team to ride the waves and create opportunities that will allow you to adjust midstream. Even in the midst of a storm, an eagle is capable of fighting while in flight. Never give up and soar above!
In building a brand and delivering a value proposition through the brand, it is not only the marketing who are involved, but the entire organization too.

When the people have begun to relate to the brand and the organization through the brand, it becomes imperative that the organization focus on delivering incremental value consistently throughout the brand.
Successful brands help to establish a relationship with the customer. Customer can be loyal to a particular brand for their lifetime. Over a period of time, the brand value and promise including the characteristics, the visual logo as well as the product offering needs to be changed keeping in line with the markets as well as the Organizational strategy for growth and direction.

At all times, the brand image should be relevant to the current times and yet conducive towards the future as well. As the brand communicates to the customer, it becomes a powerful tool that needs to be managed consciously by the Organization. Sales and Marketing career is highly rewarding both in terms of rewards as well as knowledge and experience.

Those who have a flare for meeting people and selling products or services will find it rewarding to build a sales plan, identify sales lead, build a pipeline of prospects and converting them as sales. To such salesmen, the sales figures and every new customer account counts. Then there are those who enjoy building marketing strategies, growing the brand and using their creative skills into building effective communication and advertising plans.

Deuteronomy 11:1-3 *You shall therefore love the Lord your God and keep his charge, his statutes, his rules, and his commandments always. And consider today (since I am not speaking to your children who have not known or seen it), consider the discipline of the Lord your God, his greatness, his mighty hand and his outstretched arm, his signs and his deeds that he did in Egypt to Pharaoh the king of Egypt and to all his land.*

THE GREAT AHA MOMENT

Branding yourself and your business should come naturally to you as it is a fiber of your being. Now is the time to make a move and to make your mark.

Within these chapters we have touched on a few basic guidelines that will set you well on your way.

Here is your AHA MOMENT GUIDE for useful tips to implement daily towards your journey.

A few of my go-to methods on how to brand yourself effectively:

1. Find commonalities and own them.

It would be great if you could identify certain key attributes that are common between you and your company. Once you figure those out, you can proactively work towards aligning the two in the eyes of your customers, making a strong association and owning that quality.

Every product or service has certain impressions associated with them such as honesty, effectiveness, customer focus and customer satisfaction which are important to the customers.

Identify these characteristics and incorporate them into your identity.

2. Be the expert.

You need to ensure that you lead your field and show your competitors how it is supposed to be done. Leave such a trail of excellence from tremendous effort that your competition is constantly playing catch up. If you can keep up with this, it will make you come across as a trustworthy innovator and a thought leader, making you more influential with time. It will place you in a position as someone who can identify and fill gaps in the market better than anyone else.

Your customers will perceive you as the one who cares enough to meet those needs, which were not being met before.

3. Network better.

Networking with the right people will put you in the right situations of the industry go-getters, as well as the potential customers. It is crucial that you think of a networking strategy that works for you. And irrespective of the strategy, keep in mind the law of reciprocity: When you connect with people and exchange ideas and information without worrying about who is paying you and when, the generosity will come back to you manifold.

4. Use social media.

It's easy, interesting and quick. Most of all, your customers are on it. So you should be on it, too. Be cautious of the content you place on your social media outlets, it can either earn you a fan group or cost you your business. Is your brand reflective of your lifestyle?

 Is it a business page that you should focus on branding vs your personal page? What message are you presenting to your clientele base?

5. Be a great communicator.

Not only will having excellent communication skills portray you as an effective leader, they will also help you stand out. Watch what you say, learn to write better and mind your grammar and spellings.
Work on your presentation skills; they're extremely critical for an entrepreneur, especially a successful one. If you can present well, you and your organization will be perceived as more effective.

Advertisement is the main push for any brand or business no matter what type it is. Being in the advertisement business for many years helped me gain clients all over the country. With the buzz of the social media engine, I can advertise my business to gain more trust in my clients as potential clients who wants to gain the same kind of success or more since the possibilities are endless as to what you could achieve through building and with the power of advertisement will show that it is possible and will bring you countless clients with the visions of their dreams coming into fruition.

The realization that this won't happen overnight will give you the ability to see the vision, yet stay encouraged while embarking upon the journey. It takes the consistency of promotions with every product you have on the market, with no less promotions with just one product. You want it all to be successful advertisement which would drive your brand marketing where you hoped it would be. Never underestimate your brand.

It exemplifies who and what you are. Once you begin to see it all come together, the feeling of knowing all of your hard work is paying off will ignite a fire to burn brighter. Over the years of continuously building and branding, I found it easier to be my own brand manager. I have built relationships with those who were my first clients.

I was in the business of communication through advertisement and both are assets to managing your brand, therefore I had mastered both skills, not only through education but also through experience over the years.

Although it worked for me, others may need extra help from the hiring of a manager but just know that you are the brand and no one can represent you better than yourself. Make sure that your manager can transfer your vision to the core of your building guidelines. No matter how many business partnerships you may have, they all must reflect as your initial brand as a whole. That is the key in keeping its value ranking appreciated over the years just as fine wine gets better with age, your brand shall as well. Ask yourself "What is the purpose of it all?"

My purpose isn't a dream of what I hope to be.. It's what I was born to be. What God has gifted to me. That is why all I do is from the heart. It is a part of me in every fiber of my genetics as a birth mark. It never fades away and is never out of mind. It's more powerful than breathing because even after our last breath our brand will carry on as the mark we left behind.

It should be the mark of hard work and dedication which signifies how giving up was never an option as it was completed and the torch passed on to the future of builders who are now inspired and motivated to leave and pass on a legacy of their own. Whatever you feel is worth starting, you should make it worth completing, for we shall only see accomplishments through completion. And we could only build hope in our future with completion of our projects. To prove that it can be done. Being that your brand is uniquely who you are, or shouldn't be hard or overthought in order to master craft and sculpt your vision as you are the representative of your masterpiece.

Deuteronomy 8:18 *But Remember the Lord your God, for it is He who gives you the ability to produce wealth, and so confirms His covenant, which He swore to your ancestors, as it is today…*

You were born with the entrepreneurial spirit.
You have it instilled within to be whatever
you choose to be with hard work and
dedication with all of the abilities granted to
you by God. Your plans are your goals and
your goals are you dreams all wrapped up into
a place within you ready to be exposed when
you decide to reveal your chosen path.

Just do it because there is no time guarantees
on anything in this life. Let's continue where
our ancestors left off at. Even those who did
not think it possible in their time still had faith
and hope for their future generations. We are
so much better equipped today. Make them
proud and start building your legacy today.
Do all things today of which you could look
back on and be proud of your
accomplishments. All things through Christ is
worthy of the efforts to please He who made
all things possible for us to achieve if we apply
ourselves. If at first we do not achieve, we
must try again, as nothing beats a failure but a
try. Some of the building blocks may fall at
times but they could always be re-stacked until
we get them in their projected order. To build
we must have structure, a plan and the
courage to build skyscrapers.

LEAD TO THE DOTTED LINE

Mastering the art of the sale is not just about enticing potential customers to engage with your business, but about keeping them moving down the sales train all the way to the contract's dotted line.

Your brand, your product your services has their attention, but is that enough to seal the deal? Is it enough to bring them back? Within this sales channels, many businesses get lost. While they are able to generate qualified leads, they aren't able to transform those potential customers into actual customers.

Why is that?

Successful lead engagement means creating a personal relationship with your customer. Though the days of individual, face-to-face sales may no longer be as common, those personal methods continue to be the heart of the sale. I have found that individualized approach is exactly what made modern sales successful.

Technology allows us to track customer engagement and to focus efforts.

Forging that connection in a modern, heavily competitive world is a challenge; however, it's surmountable when utilizing the right techniques.

- Provide some type of value

Before everything else, there has to be value for your customers. This is the beginning of the sale process. You need them to see the value in what you have to offer, something that they want, something that they need. The value proposition can be so obvious to businesses that they don't think it through, but crafting it carefully is the critical first step in successful lead engagement.

Are you offering a way to make life better? A way to make it easier? Does your product remove something negative in the life of your customers or add something positive? Are you taking the time to become an honorary employee of the client?

Become so engulfed with what makes their ship sail that you are capable of navigating through unforeseen storms that may cause a ripple in the original right of way.

Learn their business from the daily challenges to the company's goals and create a lane to help them get there.

The other side of providing value is giving your potential customers the content they want in the format that they need. For some customers, that might be an actual direct mail piece. Keep in mind, everyone is not on the digital wave. Some clients may better be reached by emails or in the form of a mobile app that they can download to their phone. Video content is ideal for many potential clients. If what you're giving them is the right content or the right product but in the wrong format, then it's not giving them the value that they need. It's about the whole package.

Leviticus 25:43 *You shall not rule over him ruthlessly but shall fear your God.*

- Offer information

Information is power and comfort. One key to engaging potential customers is to offer them as much information about the process as you possibly can. Realize that while your team might be intensely familiar with the processes of your company, but potential customers are very not and may need additional information in order to grasp a complete understanding of the process.
Do not wait for potential leads to come to you with questions or concerns, especially when it comes to things like timeline, delivery and managing potential problems. Always be the first to reach out when you have new information. Keeping customers informed shows you are invested in them and it is truly a collaborative effort that is offering them a sense that they are a valued part of the process and not just another number on a sales chart.

A simple email is sufficient to keep potential customers in the loop, though whatever form of communication you have established is appropriate. Just be transparent, available and informative step by step.

- Maintain integrity

Honesty is an essential part of this process and of any successful relationship. There is never a good reason to offer customers or potential customers anything that could be misleading. It's a solid rule for businesses to make a commitment to honesty and integrity no matter what problems may arise or what kinds of issues could come up.

This goes especially for claims about the efficacy of a product and the timeline of delivery. Do not over promise and under deliver an offer to a customer and do not hold back when it comes to saying what the process actually is. You will never be sorry for telling the truth to a client, but any kind of falsehood that casts shadows of doubts will come back negatively, damaging not only potential leads but also current customers.

- Create an enjoyable experience

Look to the overall experience that you are creating for potential leads. Run yourself through the process that you are offering to potential customers and think about what improvements you could make to it. Be honest with yourself. Keep it simple. Keep it consistent.
What kind of responses does your process elicit? Where are the gaps in the experience? Was there a part of the process that left you feeling uneasy? Often, there are obvious weak links that can be mended in order to keep the overall experience unified and compelling for potential customers. Identify the weak link, address the issue, correct the issue and move forward with a fine tuned machine.

Proverbs 16:18 *Pride goes before destruction, a haughty spirit before a fall.*

• Customize your approach

As you work to create that ultimate experience, be sure to meet your leads where they are. At what point are they in the sales lane? Are they researching? Ready to buy? Your customer engagement efforts should not be the same for someone who is making a first inquiry about your product as for someone who has previously been connected to you.

Lead engagement is all about the personalized, individual experience that you are offering to your customers. One of the best ways to give them the gratitude is to amend your message to meet them where they are.

The common thread through these tips for improving conversion rate is that they all move toward building that positive and personal relationship with the customer. It starts from the very beginning and moves through the whole process, bringing you to the end result that you're looking for leading them to the dotted line.

Genesis 31:6 *You know that I have served your father with all my strength*

- Display Self-Confidence

Display self-confidence, showing your coworkers your passion towards reaching the company's goals and encouraging others to do the same. Be a momentum builder. A leader of the pack will lead with style, grace , encouragement and understanding. Setting personal goals of enhancing your brand while empowering the unit as a whole. Be the beacon of light that shines bright and sets the example.

- Strive to do more

Strive to complete each task on time.
Strive to be a team player on all levels with the goal of winning in mind.
Strive to recruit and nurture team members that will assist in taking your brand to the next level.
Always have a sense of humility. It is okay to admit your flaws as none of us are perfect but do not focus on them and make your flaws a hindrance .
Show your human side but never lose your self-assurance. You are ready to level up!

- Exercise your patience

Have patience with your staff, co-workers and clients. Each will have their individual level of learning, adapting or even approaching situations. Position yourself with the nurturing approach to help them through. For coworkers, show them how to work methods of expanding the brand through hard work and dedication. For clients, show them the upside of taking the challenge of branding their businesses and becoming market leaders. People are more likely to trust and respect those who treat them well. Form a winning team. Instill the winning attitude as a characteristic of your brand.

- Whispering Winds

Be cautious of the words you place in the wind. Word travels a lot faster than you think. The market place becomes smaller and more familiar with every sales call, with every one-on-one and every transferring client or co-worker.

Do NOT get caught up in the industry's gossip. Take the time to spread the gospel of how dedicated your company is to work towards meeting the goals of clients. Let that be the resounding message traveling through the atmosphere on your end. Do not let your success become overshadowed by the gloom of unworthy gossip. Clients and co-workers need to understand that we are not in the market of branding the random chitter chatter of the "He Said, She Said" water cooler talk.

Romans 12:2 *Do not conform to the pattern of this world, but be transformed by the renewing of your mind. Then you will be able to test and approve what God's will is--his good, pleasing and perfect will.*

Be true to who you were created to be. No one is perfect as God but we must live in words. There are many temptations to sway you but we must not let those distractions falter our course of being an honest business leader in order to keep the trust of our clients and potential clients. We must remain faithful and prayerful which is our commitment to our Creator.

His Blessings to us should never be taken for granted. We must show our gratitude in the way we live our lives. The way we treat others should be the way we'd like to be treated. To give respect we expect to gain respect and a reputation that your brand would be proud of. Clients are often referred to those who are great servants of the Lord as they feel confident in trusting your business to serve them.

II Corinthians 9:8 *And God is able to bless you abundantly, so that in all things at all times, having all that you need, you will abound in every good work.*

The gift of having the gift is to appreciate the gift. To never misuse or appreciate the gift and most importantly is to share the gift to all who are inspired and realize that they too have the gift. The gift of their own unique brand which they were born with. We are not to be selfish with our gifts. We must all build together and rejoice in each other's success.

There is such a tear in the world due to selfishness which is not pleasing to God as we are all sisters and brothers in Christ and we must always help build each other up in order to make it to Him in our eternity.

There are many scammers who want to make a quick buck and will target those who they feel are weak, and attempt to sell them a false dream. We must beware of those demons that are swarming. That's why we must research before any business transaction. Read reviews and check Better Business Bureau reports before investing in any business for any project. Remember that you are the power behind your brand.

Mark 5:36 *Overhearing what they said, Jesus told them, "Don't be afraid; just believe."*

We so often hear, if only we believe, then we could achieve. Well that is the truth. That is our power of the mind to set our goals in motion. That's when it's okay to be bold and go for it.

Step out on faith because all things are possible through Christ who strengthens us. He gave us strong will and determination to use as He guide us through the obstacles we must face in life. We must trust and believe in Him and fear no one but Him.

Ecclesiastes 11:4 *He who observes the wind [and waits for all conditions to be favorable] will not sow, and he who regards the clouds will not reap.*

Always expect the unexpected and prepare regardless because no situation is ever perfect but that doesn't mean that it can't be done successfully. Some of the best things created were done so under pressure or at the last minute.
 It isn't a good way to practice doing things but it may just happen at times as being a perfectionist has stalled many projects as they feel it's never good enough to push through when in all actually it is just fine. Then all of the time stalled labels one as a procrastinator since you're constantly saying it will get done while you still hadn't produced or allowed the push through that's on hold due to you being a perfectionist.

A great business constantly and consistently produces in a manner which satisfies their clients.

Isaiah 1:17-19 *Learn to do good; seek justice, correct oppression; bring justice to the fatherless, plead the widow's cause. "Come now, let us reason together, says the Lord: though your sins are like scarlet, they shall be as white as snow; though they are red like crimson, they shall become like wool. If you are willing and obedient, you shall eat the good of the land;*

BE A BRAND THAT CARES

Proverbs 19:17 *Whoever is generous to the poor lends to the Lord, and he will repay him for his deed.*

Through all of my business brands and clients I've ever mentored, I've encouraged them to set aside a fund for charitable organizations. Giving back is the greatest feeling in your soul.

My strongest attribute has always been the ability to put people first.

It was not taught to me through text book, nor trial and error, but through the consistency of seeing my grandfather, the late Reverend Jesse Lafayette, Sr. display it within his daily routine. Putting people and their needs first. Being compassionate enough to identify the areas that needed attention to detail and derive a plan to make things better than I found them. All while being so effective with the approach it passed the need to do the same on to those who were a part of the experience.

The brand is more than the company. It is the executive team's and the individual employees' personal brands as well. People do business with people. A strong CEO brand, executive brand, or personal brand helps build a positive reputation overall.
Nearly everyone prefers working with businesses that are people-oriented and actually care about their customers.
 Be that company by embodying a people-first attitude in all that you and your employees do. Never underestimate the power of compassion. Living in a society that is fast paced, incentive driven and fueled by instant gratification; it is important to remember your WHY.

Remember WHY you started;

Remember WHY your brand is set apart from the rest;
Remember WHY you chose to stick it out and see it through;
Etch your brand within the fiber of something that is bigger than sales. Embed your brand as a part of the greater good.

Enhance the quality of life and the world we live in through an effort of giving back as a "thank you" to those who have inspired, supported and assisted you along the way. Encourage team work within your brand.

James 2:26 *Faith without works is dead.*

Understanding that it is indeed a collaborative effort and that all entities are equally important within the growth and longevity thereof.

Leviticus 23:22 *And when you reap the harvest of your land, you shall not reap your field right up to its edge, nor shall you gather the gleanings after your harvest. You shall leave them for the poor and for the sojourner: I am the Lord your God.*

Workers enjoy being praised. Notice and acknowledge them for their attention to detail, their creativity, ability to adapt and endless hours they put in to ensure the message is being etched into history one day at a time.

A simple "Thank you", will keep them encouraged and energized to see the tasks through.
Share the knowledge you have learned along the way. Speak to others within your industry on behalf of your testimony of branding your brand. Not only is this an act of the great give back, but it shows you have the confidence in the lessons learned that there actually were lessons to be learned!
Make every day a day of learning something new. Make every day a day of enlightenment.

Remember your WHY and from there let it continuously be your source of motivation to give it your all each and every day.
Show the world what you are made of and share the greatness.

You were born a brand!

Deuteronomy 15:13-14.. *And when you let him go free from you, you shall not let him go empty-handed. You shall furnish him liberally out of your flock, out of your threshing floor, and out of your winepress. As the Lord your God has blessed you, you shall give to him.*

<u>NOTES</u>

ABOUT THE AUTHOR

LaTangela is aware of what it takes to help business owners achieve their business and financial dreams. She has spent nearly twenty years helping companies with sales, strategic planning, acquisitions, human resources, operations management and training. She has extensive experience in working with business executives to successfully identify and analyze business problems, define and implement solutions. She is a Public Relations and Life coach expert who has empowered many with her motivational speaking, leadership seminars and conferences. She is in great demand with extensive client referrals due to her consistency and effectiveness. She works across a broad spectrum of industries and businesses, including a few within the Fortune 500 realm to help each company focus and energize their vision to move their business to the next phase. She also helps to create retirement and transition exit plans. Throughout her career, she has demonstrated the ability to achieve positive results in both top of the line revenues and bottom line profits. She has helped build numerous businesses in many areas of manufacturing, retail, and professional services as well as created and grew those businesses to great profits as well as helped many cut unprofitable business paths and expand their client base. LaTangela's other literary publications are: "A-Z, Lord Let It Define Me" and "Soul Inspirations". She's also a radio personality, a singer/songwriter, with numerous musical projects, and is the Founder/CEO of a production/media and recording company. LaTangela is a graduate of Southern Baptist Seminary of Theology and Philosophy with studies in Business Management and Marketing.

She resides in Baton Rouge, La.
www.430Status.com